WHO WOULD JESUS VOTE FOR?

WHO WOULD JESUS VOTE FOR?

Philip J. Gentlesk

LIBERTY HILL PRESS

Liberty Hill Press
2301 Lucien Way #415
Maitland, FL 32751
407.339.4217
www.libertyhillpublishing.com

Printed in the United States of America.

Edited by Liberty Hill Press.

Paperback ISBN-13: 978-1-6322-1401-0
Hard Cover ISBN-13: 978-1-6322-1402-7
Ebook ISBN-13: 978-1-6322-1403-4

TABLE OF CONTENTS

CHAPTER ONE

THE END OF AN ERA

I n just a few weeks, people across America will go to the polls to vote in the 2020 general election.

We will be able to decide whether Donald Trump will serve another four years as President of the United States, or if Joe Biden will take his place. (As I began to write this, singer Kanye West announced that he is also running for office, but I doubt if Messrs. Trump and Biden are too worried about that.) We'll also be able to vote for Senators and Representatives, both on the national and local levels, and a wide variety of initiatives, referendums and so on. Frankly, the choices can be bewildering, and it can be difficult to decide who and what to vote for.

Making proper decisions can be especially difficult for the hundreds of thousands of young Americans who will be voting for the first time. It is for them that I am writing this book. Not only for the youngest voters, but for all those who may feel overwhelmed by the issues and personalities involved in the 2020 election.

My intention is to help you sort out the right from wrong, the good from the bad, from a Christian perspective.

Basically, I want to tell you, from my perspective, how I think Jesus would vote.

As a concerned husband, father and business owner and – most importantly, as a follower of Christ, the future of this country is extremely important to me. I want to make sure she is headed in the direction God wants her to move in – and I'm sure you do, too.

My earliest memory of anything political takes me back to the 1952 election between Dwight Eisenhower and Adlai Stevenson. As late October approached, the promise of a sackful of candy, carved pumpkins, and other seasonal trappings loomed large in the minds of every young kid in America. Yet, even more so, my friends and I were curious about who would be the next president. Excitement permeated my grammar school, though we didn't have a clue what all the hubbub meant.

We were just kids, and my mind was focused for the most part on the stats being put up by Philadelphia Eagles quarterback, Bobby Thompson. I'm embarrassed to say I had nothing to offer any conversation. With the election only a few days away, it was time to ask Dad what he thought.

The boring walk home from school was particularly chilly. Fallen leaves and countess acorns peppered the normally tidy yards. Against the monotonous backdrop of late fall in New Jersey, bright orange pumpkins stood sentry on every stoop. The aroma of supper welcomed me at the front door to my house. The screen door slamming behind me, I greeted Mom and plopped down at the carefully set kitchen table.

"Time for dinner, son, so go wash up! And where is my hug?" Without grumbling or complaining, I did as I was told.

By the time I was presentable for dinner, Dad and my siblings had arrived and were seated at the table. Mom, proudly flaunting her Italian heritage, served homemade pasta with traditional meats. We said grace before digging into the most delicious food ever created. Pleasant conversation and a sense of family, common to the era, provided as much nourishment as Mom's amazing cooking. Somewhere between "pass the meatballs" and more compliments to the chef, I posed the election question.

The table fell silent, and all faces turned toward me in surprise. The nature of the query didn't shock anyone, but the fact that the question had come from me did. Until that moment, sports had been my only topic of interest.

After the brief shock, Dad smiled and declared, almost reverently, he would be voting for Dwight D. Eisenhower. He made a few mild comments about things I didn't understand, but I did conclude he didn't think Eisenhower's opponent, Adlai Stevenson, was the right choice for our family.

While my parents weren't particularly political, I learned over the years that my father was an Independent voter. He put family first, and the candidate whose values supported the family always won Dad's vote. Mom, on the other hand, was generally disinterested unless there was some movement afoot to raise grocery prices. They were just proud to be Americans.

With more information in my arsenal, I joined the election chats at school. Eisenhower won the presidency by a massive margin, his victory ending a long stretch of leadership for the Democratic Party. During Eisenhower's presidency, party differences were about issues, not personalities.

As he campaigned for the presidency, Adlai Stevenson's game plan was to instill fear in the American public by proclaiming a Republican win would bring about another Great Depression.

The America of my youth wasn't immune to political posturing and certainly had its share of drama. But, beneath it all, one could still detect an undercurrent of integrity. We were not bombarded by character assassinations, media bias, or inflammatory footage of angry mobs intent on violence, arson, or looting.

While we definitely had our issues and problems, the America I fondly remember also had much to be admired. Neighbors helped each other, doors were left unlocked, doctors made house calls, milk was delivered to your door, and merchants with horse-drawn food carriages offered fresh produce.

Sadly, things have changed considerably since those days.

Modern America has become a place I could never have imagined. Amidst a minefield of contempt, many are no longer free to voice their true opinions. A new breed of "back-office globalists," who attempt to understand the modern world, believes that people, goods, and information should cross all borders, unfettered. It's good only if you are a giant corporate entity or a huge bank as it permits them to use their leverage against anyone or any country.

The apparent drift of our Christian country toward atheism is most concerning. According to the Barna Group, Christianity in the United States has declined from 81 percent in 2003 to 72 percent in 2018. Several emerging trends continue to impact these statistics. Young people approaching adulthood are losing interest in any form of religion. In my opinion, they have a new god: themselves.

Not surprisingly, atheism has grown in the wake of evangelism's decrease. Millennials, nearly half of whom neither want nor support any type of evangelism, go even further and believe evangelism itself is wrong.

In addition, the birth of socialism in America could likely pave the way for advocates of communism. Anyone thinking this couldn't happen shouldn't be so sure. The young "woke" youth of our country want everything for nothing and have no concept of earning. The tragedy of this rationale is that

Millennials believe they themselves – and the United States – are invincible. I would agree with this sentiment, if God were still part of the equation.

Tragically, this new America has told God He is no longer necessary. Citizens have rebelled against the Christian values upon which our nation was founded. We have taken prayer out of our schools, condoned abortion, and supported acts God calls abominations. We are already feeling the consequences of these actions.

It is difficult to deny the rising occurrence of earthquakes, forest fires, floods, riots, border skirmishes, and now, the unthinkable development of a global pandemic.

Historically, God has allowed these types of events to take place when His creation is in rebellion.

Bear in mind, within our society, politicians are fashioning the rules and realities. Trying to determine which party is telling us the truth is not always an easy task. Our once-reliable and patriotic media now vilifies some and aggrandizes others, and the average citizen cannot determine lies from truth. We must have access to accurate and unbiased information if we are to make good decisions.

In this book, I hope to provide insight to help us understand God's reaction to modern society. Focusing on the origins of both the Democrats and the Republicans, I will show the progression of each Party and apply God's Word to politics. By placing each Party's foundation and evolution in the light of biblical truth, one can determine a clear Christian path amid our increasingly partisan culture.

I believe that we are faced with not only a political fight but a spiritual battle. For this reason, it is important to engage the right mindset and proximity to God. The wisdom found in James 4:8 provides a solid foundation for inviting God into this exploration.

"Draw near to God, and He will draw near to you. Cleanse your hands, you sinners, and purify your hearts, you double minded."

One might think God would come to us. Instead, the opposite is true. When it comes to achieving the right spiritual disposition needed to entertain higher truths, we have to actively focus on God to receive His attention. However, as the verse suggests, it's difficult to apply such focus when our hearts are heavy with sin and our minds are riddled with indecision.

CHAPTER TWO

DON'T BELIEVE THE LIES

I'm sure I'm not the only one who has wondered why God allows political lies (and liars) to continue. Answer: God is long-suffering.

In this context, *long-suffering* doesn't mean, as the dictionary states, "showing patience in spite of troubles." God knows all things and never runs out of patience. His endurance is limitless. He doesn't want anyone to perish and, thus, His long-suffering demonstrates His love in action. In time, He will deal with every lie and every liar.

Every day each citizen in the USA is bombarded by lies and mistruths from a multitude of directions. Consider, what we (and especially our youth) would do without our cell phones and computers? We have become addicted to social media. This type of addiction has been described as a 'behavioral addiction' that negatively impacts the mental health and relationships of those addicted.

Some of the causes of this addiction are related to the nonstop notifications we all receive. With the constant interruption of distracting and unavoidable notifications, we simply cannot concentrate on whatever task we are trying to perform. This continual disruption actually causes stress, and in some cases, can even prompt anger.

Young people are perhaps the most distracted by these technologies. Sadly, they seem to care more about their social media identity than real-life interactions. They have become over-invested in the pursuit of "followers" who basically define and validate the user.

In her book, *The Happiness Effect: How Social Media is Driving a Generation to Appear Perfect at Any Cost,*[1] Donna Freitas says: "In our attempts to be happy, to distract ourselves from our deeper, sometimes darker thoughts, we experience the opposite effect. In trying to always appear happy, we rob ourselves of joy. . ." I worry that social media is teaching us that we are not worthy. That it has us living in a compulsive and perpetual loop of such feedback. That in our constant attempts to edit out our imperfections for massive public viewing, we are losing sight of the things that ground our life in connection and love, in meaning and relationships.

> "Our brave faces are draining us. We're losing
> sight of our authentic selves."

By design, intentional or not, social media platforms facilitate narcissism and delusion. Equally unsettling is the fact that social media is addictive, and one could speculate that long-term results will be devastating. Don't get me wrong. I believe in free speech. But I wish there were more discernment on the part of the American public. Far too many lies and fairy tales are being passed off as real news. And our youth are not the only ones who are being led astray. Everyone seems to be juggling social media life with real family time and personal interactions. In this balancing act, the entire family loses.

Stress develops as an unavoidable side effect of this addiction. An overabundance of time spent immersed in social media leads to loss of self-control and independence. Users begin copying behaviors observed from peers. Cyber bullying is often another consequence confronting youngsters. Victims become anxious, depressed, and, in some cases, suicidal.

Consider the consequences of your child driving to school or to a store while texting a friend. This all too common distraction has resulted in injuries and death.

Social media addiction should not be ignored. Peer approval is highly important to our young people, and they take it seriously. Children have been damaged emotionally and psychologically by unfavorable remarks made online.

Our first thought might be to take away the use of the cell phone entirely, but this is most likely not the best solution. Perhaps, to earn the use of the phone each day, you can have the child read a few verses of Scripture on a Bible app and discuss it together. For example:

> "So My word that proceeds from My mouth will not return to Me empty, but it will accomplish what I please, and it will prosper where I send it."
> (Isaiah 55:11)

Understanding the above verse as we analyze our present political situation can help us grasp how these many distractions in life have caused us to be oblivious to the reality of the media and its influence on our American way of life. We must not allow ourselves to fall prey to the political distractions propagated by the liberal media.

Understanding one's beliefs is important in determining how one votes. Does your thinking sync one hundred percent with what your party believes? Are their values the same as yours? It's not enough to be satisfied with most of a party's platform, but not be in agreement to their stance on immigration or abortion, and so on.

Consider how our Lord would vote on the same issues the platform espouses. Visualize the day you vote as being your last day on earth. Knowing you would be face to face with Him soon, would you change your thinking or be confident with your political position and the votes you cast?

Spend time listening to God. Meditate on His Word. Study the book of Proverbs and learn the mind of God. Filter your thoughts and questions through the wisdom in this book. It's amazing what you will learn.

CHAPTER THREE

THE BIBLICAL EMERGENCE OF POLITICS

D id God intend for human beings to form a government? Romans 13:1-2 tells us:

> "Every person is to be in subjection to the governing authorities. For there is no authority except from God, and those that exist are established by God. Therefore, whoever resists authority has opposed the ordinance of God; and they who have opposed will receive condemnation unto themselves."

And there's also this, written by the Apostle Peter: "*Submit yourselves for the Lord's sake to every human authority: whether to the emperor, as the supreme authority, or to governors, who are sent by him to punish those who do wrong and to commend those who do right. For it is God's will that by doing good you should silence the ignorant talk of foolish people. Live as free people, but do not use your freedom as a cover-up for evil; live as God's slaves. Show proper respect to everyone, love the*

family of believers, fear God, honor the emperor."
(1 Peter 2:16-17)

Do you believe the Bible is the Word of God? The most important thing in your life is your understanding of questions such as: Who am I? Where did I come from? And where am I going?

This planet we call Earth could not have just happened. Someone created it and placed it in perfect proximity to a heat source to sustain life.

Take time to research and study the following. Your conclusions determine eternal life or eternal death.

You may be one who wonders if the Bible is true and demand hard evidence. Are you in the same camp as those who believe the Scriptures are little more than ideas and folklore of ancient man? Perhaps your Western mind cannot understand the literary methods used by past civilizations, though archaeology has revealed much of this.

In essence, the Bible is a collection of many books written by multiple authors over a 1,500-year period. The first section of Scripture is the Pentateuch, or the five Books of Moses, and includes Genesis, Exodus, Leviticus, Numbers, and Deuteronomy. Genesis chronicles creation, man's rebellion, the global flood, and God's choosing of the Israelites, through which Christ, the Savior of mankind, would come.

Jesus referred to these books, also known as the Torah or the Law, when He said that Moses wrote of Him.

> *". . .and beginning at Moses and all the Prophets, He expounded unto them in all the scriptures the thing's concerning Himself ... all things must be fulfilled, which were written in the Law of Moses, and in the Prophets, and in the Psalms, concerning Me."* (Luke 24:25,27,44 NASB)

Moses kept meticulous records, recording every event, as he led Israel out of slavery in Egypt. He taught the sons of Israel Deuteronomy 31:22, a song written on "the same day" as the event.

Other references to the writings of Moses can be found in Exodus, which Moses wrote as a memorial.

> *"Then Amalek came and fought against Israel at Rephidim. So Moses said to Joshua, "Choose men for us and go out, fight against Amalek. Tomorrow I will station myself on the top of the hill with the staff of God in my hand." Joshua did as Moses told him, and fought against Amalek; and Moses, Aaron, and Hur went up to the top of the hill. So it came about when Moses held his hand up, that Israel prevailed, and when he let his hand down, Amalek prevailed. But Moses' hands were heavy. Then they took a stone and put it under him, and he sat on it; and Aaron and Hur supported his hands, one on one side and one on the other. Thus his hands were steady until the sun set. So Joshua overwhelmed Amalek and his people with the edge of the sword.*
>
> *Then the Lord said to Moses, "Write this in a book as a memorial and recite it to Joshua, that I will utterly blot out the memory of Amalek from under heaven."* (Exodus 17:8-14 NASB)

Then again, and again, Moses was instructed to 'write down all the words.' (Exodus 24:4-7; Deuteronomy 31:9-12,24-26) Numbers 33:2 tells us Moses recorded all travels of his 40 years of leadership.

"Moses recorded their starting places according to their journeys by the command of the LORD, and these are their journeys according to their starting places." (NASB)

Adopted by Pharaoh's daughter, Moses was educated in words and customs. He was more than capable to carry out the recording of history. Flavius Josephus (the first century historian who authored *Antiquities of the Jews*) wrote in 70 AD " ... but only 22 books which contain the records of all the past times; which are justly believed to be divine, and of them five belong to Moses which contain his laws and the tradition of the origins of mankind till his death." [2]

Archaeology has substantiated the customs from 2000 to 1500 B.C. as described by Moses, thereby supporting the truth and accuracy of the Torah.

God reveals Himself to His creation through the Bible. In order to confuse mankind, the devil introduced the lie of evolution. This lie persuaded man that religion evolved from Animism, which is a supernatural power that organizes and animates the material world. In other words, it is a belief that non-human entities contain souls.

In Exodus, God tells Moses that He revealed Himself to Abraham, Isaac, and Jacob as "El Shaddai," which means "God Almighty." This is the name God used to seal His covenant with the Patriarchs. The name He used to seal His covenant with the Israelites was Jehovah, which means the "Eternal One" or the "One for Whom all time is present."

Victor Pearce mentions in his book, *Origins of the Bible,* that "the use of different divine names was not an indication that they came from different sources, but followed certain principles. These principles have existed in ancient times and also in Christ's time by scribal writings, and it continues to this day.

The methods God used to convey His message to man varied. Hebrews 1:1-2 says, "God ... in diverse manners spake in time past ... Hath in these last days spoken unto us by His Son."

Think about this: the book of Genesis records events before the life of Moses. Archaeology supports the accuracy of events and cultures depicted. An example of this would be the succession of prehistoric cultures, i.e. Stone Age, Copper-stone Age, Bronze Age, Iron Age, and so on. In addition, the order of creation is the same as agreed upon by scientists.

It is written that the scribe Phinehas, who was a priest during the Israelites' exodus from Egypt and a grandson of Aaron, distinguished himself as a youth at Shittim with his zeal against the heresy of Peor, a god of the Moabites who was worshipped with obscene rites (Numbers 25:3;31:16).

His son wrote Joshua's history of the occupation of the promised land (Joshua 24:26).

Let's look at what the Prophets recorded. In each case, it is clear the writers wrote about contemporary events. The significant part is they all wrote in absolute harmony. Someone who was writing in Asia said exactly the same thing someone in Egypt said, though they were separated by time and space. This happened thousands of years ago without the benefit of the internet or any other means of communication.

The Bible records controversial issues, such as miracles. In the Old Testament, God parted the Red Sea, caused the sun to stand still, and created a fish large enough to swallow a man to name a few. In today's world, anything supernatural is dismissed as unbelievable, causing many to have doubts about the Bible. Those who do not believe in God automatically place miracles in the unreasonable box.

I assure you the Bible is true. And you may ask, "What is truth?" A dictionary gives us one definition as "a fact or belief that is accepted as true." I prefer the Focus on the Family definition saying, "Truth is what corresponds to reality, consequently, what is real is true, what is unreal is false."

The Bible makes specific claims: God is real and He communicates to us through our moral conscience and His Word. You may be asking for physical evidence proving the Bible is true.

At first glance, we can find archeological remains. Researching the *Archaeological Study Bible*, many articles document how archaeology unequivocally supports the Bible. In reviewing copies of ancient manuscripts, we find further documentation to support the accuracy and the legitimacy of the Bible.

Regardless of all the physical evidence, Jesus Christ Himself is the most important reason to believe in the integrity of the Bible. Again, quoting Focus on the Family, "[If} it can be shown that the four Gospels—Matthew, Mark, Luke and John— present an accurate record of the life and ministry of Jesus, then Jesus Himself becomes an argument in support of the truth of the Bible."

If the Bible has been shown to be reliable, this reasoning is no longer circular, but rational. In other words, what the Bible records about Jesus, including what He says about God, human nature, salvation, and the Old Testament record, can be trusted.

My friend, Hank Hanegraaff (the Bible Answer Man) says, concerning the tangible proof of the Bible, "Archaeology is a powerful witness to the accuracy of the New Testament documents. Repeatedly, comprehensive archaeological fieldwork and careful biblical interpretation affirm the reliability of the Bible."

Hank mentions the following example:

> "Archaeological finds have corroborated biblical details surrounding the trial that led to the fatal torment of Jesus Christ, including Pontius Pilate, who ordered Christ's crucifixion, as well as Caiaphas, the high priest, who presided over the religious trials of Christ. It is telling when secular scholars must revise their biblical criticisms in light of solid archaeological evidence."

Hank then goes on to say, "Finally, the Bible records predictions of events that could not be known nor predicted by chance or common sense. For example, the book of Daniel (written before 530 B.C.) accurately predicts the progression of kingdoms from Babylon through the Median and Persian empires to the further persecution and suffering of the Jews under Antiochus IV Epiphanes with his desecration of the temple, his untimely death, and freedom for the Jews under Judas Maccabaeus (165 BC)."

It is statistically preposterous that any or all of the Bible's specific, detailed prophecies could have been fulfilled through chance, good guessing, or deliberate deceit.

CHAPTER FOUR

THE REPUBLICANS

O kay, bear with me here because this can be kind of confusing.

Supporters of Thomas Jefferson adopted the word *republican* in 1792. Jefferson's philosophy, consistent with today's Republican party, favored a decentralized government with limited powers. The Democratic-Republican party, founded by Thomas Jefferson and James Madison and better known as the Republican Party, was our nation's dominant party from 1800 to 1829. Jefferson and Madison believed the Constitution to be a strict document that limited the powers of the federal government.

The Federalist Party disagreed. In fact, many of the early members of this party wanted to establish a monarchy in the United States. In 1828 the Democratic-Republican Party split into two separate groups: the Federalist National Republicans and the Democrats.

After that, there was no Republican Party in the United States until 1854 when a new political party was formed by opponents of the Kansas–Nebraska Act, which allowed for the expansion into the new western territories of the United States.

Six years later, Abraham Lincoln became the first Republican President. Under the leadership of Lincoln and a Republican

Congress, slavery was banned in the United States in 1865. Since then, there have been more Republican presidents than from any other party. In recent years, Republican presidents have included Ronald Reagan, George Bush, George W. Bush and Donald Trump.

Since 1973, when the Supreme Court's decision in *Roe v. Wade* legalized abortion, the Republican Party has had an anti-abortion plank in its platform, which has earned it the support of the vast majority of evangelical Christians.

Although there is no direct link with Thomas Jefferson's Democratic-Republican Party, there are many similarities between the two when it comes to policies – such as the desire to keep the government as small and manageable as possible.

I think it's important to say a few more words about the Republican's opposition to slavery. For most of us, *slavery* is simply a word, with the majority of today's youth having no idea what is embodied in it. In actuality, slavery predates written records and has existed in most cultures, including ancient civilizations such as Egypt, China, Assyria, Iran, Greece, India, and the Roman Empire. It is fair to say that the ancient world was filled with slavery of different types: debt slavery, prisoners of war slavery, child abandonment, and more. Children born to slaves were automatically slaves themselves.

In the Americas, the majority of slaves came from Africa where slavery was endemic, part of their everyday life, with Africans selling Africans for profit. According to historians, the first arrival of slaves, who were not considered slaves but explorers arriving with the Spanish, occurred in the early 1600s.

According to history books, the slave issue began in 1619 and ended with the 13th Amendment, lasting approximately

246 years. One shocking truth is that only twenty-five percent of southerners owned slaves. One of the many deplorable facts of slavery is that slaves were graded for sale.

According to Carol Swain (a black conservative television analyst and former professor at Vanderbilt University), the Democratic Party defended slavery, initiated the Civil War, imposed segregation, perpetrated lynching, and vigorously fought against civil rights acts in the 1950s. And they founded the KKK.

At the 1856 Republican convention, John C. Fremont was nominated on a platform that called for the abolition of slavery in the territories. He was supported by the northern states but lost his bid for the presidency.

In 1860 the Democratic Party split over the slavery issue, which allowed Abraham Lincoln to win the presidency. He captured sixty percent of the electoral vote, winning eighteen northern states. However, seven southern states seceded from the Union at his inauguration, with the Civil War soon following (1861-1865).

In January 1863, as our nation approached its third year of bloody civil war, Lincoln signed the Emancipation Proclamation. Slaves were now "forever free." This proclamation changed life in America. The Civil War was no longer about saving the Union, but about freeing all slaves as well. For this reason, Britain and France lost enthusiasm for supporting the Confederacy. Freed slaves were allowed to join the Union Army, thus increasing the North's fighting abilities and manpower by over 200,000 additional troops.

Lincoln's decree essentially disarmed the South, as the southern economy was primarily based on slavery. Three million slaves were now free. In its essence, the Emancipation Proclamation changed the battle between the North and South, which was originally regarding states' rights, into a fight for freedom. A fight the world could witness. A fight that would forever change the South and its ability to recreate an economy meaningful to its inhabitants. Georgia, South Carolina, Mississippi, Louisiana, Virginia, and North Carolina were the hardest hit and needed a new system of labor.

Five days after General Robert E. Lee surrendered at Appomattox in 1865, Lincoln was assassinated. Reconstruction would be handled by the new president, Andrew Johnson, who incidentally, was a former slave owner. The effect on the Republican Party was overwhelming. Republicans dominated Congress and ushered in "Reconstruction policies for America." During this timeframe, the 13th, 14th, and 15th Amendments to our Constitution were passed. The Republican Party would lose control of the South, but it continued to dominate the executive branch of our government, until the election of Franklin D. Roosevelt in 1933.

After 1912, the Republican Party underwent an ideological shift to the right. Following the Civil Rights Act of 1964 and the Voting Rights Act of 1965, the core shifted. Southern states became more Republican in Presidential elections, believing individuals should take responsibility for their own actions and that the private sector is more effective in helping the poor through charity rather than through government welfare.

From the tax side historically, Republicans lower taxes to benefit business, while Democrats raise taxes to fund social programs.

Republicans favor tariffs to protect and encourage American workers.

Both parties strongly believe in education. Republicans tend to be, by nature, conservative and support free-market capitalism, free enterprise, a strong national defense, deregulation, and conservative values based on a Christian foundation.

They are opposed to abortion, opposed to funding Planned Parenthood groups, drugs, the Affordable Care Act, gun control, and the estate tax.

The Republican Party seems to remain split on immigration.

An Overview of the Republican Platform

Rejects Supreme Court ruling on same-sex marriage. Defends marriage as between a man and a woman

Calls for building a wall on our southern border

Calls for proof of citizenship and voter ID cards in order to vote in elections

Favors the repeal of federal restrictions on campaign contributions

In favor of replacing family planning programs with abstinence

Favors overturning Roe vs Wade by naming conservative judges to the Supreme Court

Opposes restrictions of gun rights

In favor of opening federal lands to expanding oil exploration

Generally opposed to the separation of Church and State

CHAPTER FIVE

THE DEMOCRATS

What is a Democrat? Is it a supporter of democracy? Yes, of course. However, in the United States the word Democrat also means a member of the Democratic Party. This is a loaded definition as there are many parties, both domestically and internationally, that support democracy as a fundamental principle.

In the United States, parties like the Republican and Libertarian parties are by definition democratic. However, there seems to be a bias among the academic brain-trust, with many "scholars" attaching democracy exclusively to the Democratic Party. The current Democratic Party, according to some dictionaries, emphasizes egalitarianism and social equality through liberalism. These noble concepts are not exclusively related to the Democratic Party. The pursuits of equality, social justice, environmental stewardship, and general fairness are God-given to every human being. These are basic moral values that transcend politics and party allegiances.

Although some Democrats claim their party can trace its roots all the way back to Thomas Jefferson and his Democratic-Republican Party, I believe it is more accurate to say that the modern Democratic Party was founded in 1828 by Andrew Jackson and his supporters. From the beginning, the Democrats saw themselves as the party for everyday people. The Democrats are the oldest voter-based political party in the world, and the oldest existing political party in the United States.

In its early years, the party stood for individual rights, state sovereignty, and opposed ideas such as national banks and the abolition of slavery.

In 1830, the Whig Party was formed to oppose President Andrew Jackson and the Democrats. Members of the Whig Party included Henry Clay, Daniel Webster, William Henry Harrison, Zachary Taylor, and many others. The Whigs believed in protective tariffs, national banking, and federal aid programs for internal improvements.

The original Whig Party was really the party of Abraham Lincoln, whereas the Democratic Party's founding fathers were men like Martin Van Buren and, as I've already mentioned, Andrew Jackson.

Today's modern version of the Democratic Party originated with Franklin D. Roosevelt (FDR) in 1932. The Party dominated with its new, progressive liberal policies and programs in the New Deal coalition, combating bank closings and ongoing depression since the stock market crash in 1929.

The embers of the liberal ideals we see today were sparked by President Roosevelt in the 1930s. The New Deal Coalition and the new liberal idealism were founded on the alignment of interest groups and voting blocs in the United States that supported the New Deal. The New Deal Coalition supported such programs as the Civilian Conservation Corps (CCC), Civil Works Administration (CWA), the Farm Security Administration (FSA), and the Social Security Administration (SSA).

The power of the coalition ensured the election of Democratic presidents from 1932 through the 1960s. The Party lost only once, to Dwight D. Eisenhower, a pro-New Deal Republican.

The large-scale government programs were successful under FDR but began to fall apart amid the pressure of factionalism during the 1968 election. Not surprisingly, this is the type of model that today's Democrats seek passionately. They long for the lasting dominance and control they have been desperately missing since the heyday of the New Deal coalition.

Today's Democratic Party is forcing the ideas of universal voting, including superfluous LGBTQ rights that infringe on heterosexual rights, social benefits for non-citizens, and religious secularism. In my opinion, the moral compass forged by God and given to mankind has been shattered and discarded by the new Democrats.

The modern Democratic Party is certainly not the Party of its fondly remembered champion, John F. Kennedy. Today's Party describes itself as supporting American Liberalism and American Progressives, as well as the more left-wing movements such as "Social Democracy" and "Democratic Socialism." Even the so-called conservative Democratic ideology is vastly different from the conservative policies supported by the Republican Party.

In the past, the gap wasn't as wide and cooperation was more common. Today's Democrats tend to facilitate damaging social agendas, such as non-citizen equality, abortion, and the expansion of identity politics. All of these raise serious concern for our country's spiritual and financial future. It is extremely difficult and frustrating to witness Party contemporaries such as Adam Schiff, Chuck Schumer, and Jerry Nadler using questionable tactics to advance anti-conservative thinking. Anyone with a sense of the way things were, or having discernment of how things should be, registers a deep uneasiness when exposed to such divisive partisan behavior.

The Democratic Party today would view former President Kennedy as a Reaganite extremist. Based on my memory of the late Kennedy, I wouldn't be surprised if he would probably renounce the Democratic Party of 2020. According to Washington Times writer, Stephen Moore, the Democratic Party has fallen.

Think about this: A little over 30 years ago Democrat Senator Bill Bradley, house leader Dick Gephardt, and the late Jack Kemp sponsored a bill slashing the tax rate to twenty-eight percent. They worked side by side with President Reagan to get the top rate of fifty percent down to twenty-eight percent and closed many loopholes in the system.

The Bradley bill cut the highest rate to twenty-seven percent. This was accomplished with the support of most of the liberal senators, such as Ted Kennedy, Howard Metzenbaum, and Al Gore. They supported reform movement, trading low tax rates for removal of tax shelters for the very rich. The 1986 tax reform bill was a bipartisan achievement.

Fast forward to 2020 and almost all the leading Democrat candidates endorse a return to higher taxes to restore fairness for the middle class and to promote social justice. The Republicans, on the other hand, support free-market capitalism, free enterprise, business, a strong national defense, deregulation, restrictions on labor unions, social conservative policies, and traditional values based on Christian fundamentals.

Then we have another player in the game who stands for Democratic Socialism. This is a political group that supports economic and social interventions in an effort to promote social justice within the framework of a Liberal Democratic Party and a capitalist-oriented economy.

Social democrats believe that our capitalist system is inherently evil and must be reformed. Democratic Socialists advocate changing from capitalism to socialism.

Then comes the far left, which is communism. Socialism at its core is an economic philosophy, whereas communism is economic and political in its requirement that government be the central owner and decision maker in all matters.

It is beyond my comprehension how our country can entertain the principles of socialism and communism after having fought so long and hard and lost so many lives to obtain and preserve our liberty.

President Kennedy said, "It is a paradoxical truth that tax rates are too high today and tax revenues are too low," and suggested that the best way to handle this is to cut taxes. Paraphrasing, an economy constrained by high tax rates will never produce enough revenue to balance the budget, just as it will never create enough jobs or enough profits.

During Obama's administration, we received higher tax rates on most all federal taxes. The tax rate for capital gains increased by nearly sixty percent, the same rate for corporate dividends. Income tax for the disfavored increased by twenty percent. In other words, the sources for American jobs were severely impacted. Obama also restored the death tax, which Congress had voted to phase out. Capital investment is the source of new jobs in our capitalist society. Mr. Obama never understood this principle.

Obama's economic policies were consistently anti-growth. He proposed another trillion-dollar increase in personal and corporate taxes in his 2015 budget proposal. The overregulation and destabilization of monetary policies were the hallmark of his administration.

In my estimation, the Democrats are no longer the Party of the common man. They believe in giving away our hard-earned money to people who are looking for a free ride. They do not believe in a country where we all do our share. In my opinion, "pay your share" is not too much to ask.

Barack Obama: Thoughts on Socialism

Ken Blackwell, former Ohio Secretary of State, now a conservative commentator, said, "My fundamental belief is that he (Barack Obama) wants to transform our market economy into a government-controlled economy–not far afield from European-style socialism."

That said, I do not think (based on the definition of a socialist) that Obama is a socialist in the true sense of the word. What he is, however, is a 'nexus between industry and political power,' with his policies growing from his socialist associates.

Stanley Kurtz, in his book, *Radical-in-Chief: Obama and the Untold Story of American Socialism,* [3]says that President Obama is a personable figure, a thoughtful politician, and an inspiring orator. Obama has hidden his core political beliefs from the American people, sometimes by omitting damaging information to disguise its real importance. Obama presents himself as a post-ideological pragmatist, yet his policies represented a more socialistic slant on life, which, as mentioned, were gleaned from his globalist peers.

I believe supporting today's Democratic platform is essentially saying, "God, we don't care what You say. We're going to do what we want!"

Regarding homosexuality, I would like to make an important point abundantly clear. As a body of believers, we hate the sin but love the sinner. There is little chance of convincing anyone who is gay to simply change their mind. We must pray that their ears will be opened to the truth of Scripture, that they will want the truth. Down deep, I believe man's nature recognizes that God does not make mistakes nor does He lie. His plan does not include homosexuality or gender change. To say otherwise would be calling God a liar. And He never would have said "Be fruitful and multiply" (Genesis 1:28). Anyone who wants God must look for Him. He knows your heart; He knows your motives. He will find you effortlessly.

Let's take a closer look at some of the areas where Republicans differ:

The Economy

Democrats believe in building the economy from the middle out, while Republicans believe in top-down economics.

In other words, Republicans look first at the big picture. After they have taken a macro view of the economy as it relates to assessing our military readiness, our investment in keeping the USA safe and free, then they look at the smaller factors in finer details. Those details include free-market capitalism, gun rights, restrictions on abortion, and supporting lower taxes just to name a few. This top-down approach to economics prioritizes macroeconomics or market-level factors.

The Democrats middle-out approach identifies the buying power of the middle class as the most important ingredient for job creation and economic growth. In other words, Democrats claim that a strong middle class is the cause of growth rather than the consequence of it.

Anything Goes

Democrats of today tend to support the illogical expansion of voting groups, rights for illegal immigrants, and unfounded benefits for alternative subcultures. Regrettably, these agendas weaken the cornerstone on which this country was established.

It's not difficult to imagine the long-term financial and spiritual damage of advancing reckless inclusion for the sake of expanding party numbers. To gain a true sense of where this is all going, it's important to look to the past

Certainly, the Democratic Party has come a long way from its more authentic and perhaps nobler version of the Fifties and Sixties. Arguably, the Party was useful and easily understood, even by Republicans of the time.

The 2020 updated and reenergized Democratic Party would be unrecognizable to the Democratic Party of the Fifties and Sixties. I am convinced that today's social liberal platform is shameful to Almighty God. Early Party members in the Fifties were conservative, pro-labor, and of higher moral character. Today everyone wants something for nothing.

"Anything goes" seems to be the Democratic Party's battle cry. I believe most folks who subscribe to the Democratic Party are good, hardworking people who are clueless as to the path they are traveling. The Democratic website states, "We are fighting for a better, fairer, and brighter future for every American: rolling up our sleeves, empowering grassroots voters, and organizing everywhere to take our country back."

What kind of future do you want for your children and your grandchildren? Do you want them to live in the country today's Democratic Party is trying so hard to create?

It is appalling to think what our children are permitted to do. Don't like your gender? Change it! The Democratic web page on civil rights declares, "Democrats will always fight to end discrimination on race, ethnicity, national origin, language, religion, gender, age, sexual orientation, gender identity, or disability."

Parents of America, it's time to step up and fulfill your most important task: tell your children the truth. At the end of the day, no matter how much money you have, no matter how politically connected you are, no matter who you know, if you have not given your children Christ you have failed. Give your children a chance. Choose life.

In the January, 2020 edition of the Prophetic Observer, Pastor Larry Spargimino states, "The lying left has a clear agenda for American youth. The creation of a godless mob of confused people who aren't sure if they are male, female, or 29 other possibilities. They want a population without moral principles, morbid, hopeless, drugged, whimpering automatons programmed to cave in to the dictates of a God-hating new world order." [4]

This new world order sees children as means to an end. Destroy the family and you will destroy America.

Would Jesus vote for easy access to abortions? Remember, He told His disciples that anyone who wanted to enter the kingdom of God must have the simple faith of a child. He also said that if anyone caused a child to stumble, "it would be better for them to have a large millstone hung around their neck and to be drowned in the depths of the sea." (Matthew 18:6)

Would Jesus cast His vote for an organization that supports gay marriage? He clearly viewed marriage as being between one man and one woman.

Because of these two issues alone, it seems clear that Jesus would not be able to cast His vote for the Democratic Party.

Democratic Party Action Points:

Relaxed immigration
Expanded voting rights
Campaign finance reform
Universal healthcare
Stricter gun control laws
Climate change action

Increase the minimum wage
Increased capital gains tax
Tax cuts for low and middle class
Provision of preschool education
Free college education
Electoral reform
Support for same-sex marriages
Legal access to abortion

CHAPTER SIX

THE LIBERAL AGENDA

I f you believe in God and plan to vote in the next election, you should explore the intentions of your party. There are spiritual consequences to your allegiance, and believing in God requires a deep, abiding faith in His Word.

Job 34; 16-20 puts it this way, *"But if you have understanding, hear this; Listen to the sound of my words. Shall one who hates justice rule? And will you condemn the righteous mighty One, who says to a king, worthless one, to nobles, wicked ones, who shows no partiality to princes nor regards the rich above the poor, for they all are the work of His hands? In a moment they die, and at midnight people are shaken and pass away, and the mighty are taken away without a hand."*

Verse 21 concludes with this: *"For His eyes are upon the ways of a man, and He sees all his steps."*

In addition to this abiding faith, there must be an understanding of what's going on in this world and how contemporary events apply to our spiritual journey. Isaiah presents a timely overlay in 54:16 (NASB):

"Behold I myself have created the smith who blows the fire of coals and brings out a weapon for its work; And I have created the destroyer to ruin. No weapon that is formed against you will

prosper; and every tongue that accuses you in judgement you will condemn."

The "smith" refers to manufacturers of instruments of war and torture. The torture instruments are references to peacetime persecutions. Basically, through these two examples we learn that, while God is entirely in control, the faithful must be aware of injustice and stand against movements to downgrade His authority.

Presently, designs to replace God are unfolding in deviously subtle ways. The political arena brims with individuals who despise sharing the stage with God so much that they fabricate and propagate lies. Whether they themselves believe in God or not, they observe the obedience of God's followers and envy the power. Of course, God will deal with them as He has with many other political leaders throughout time. However, in the meantime, believers should remain vigilant. To assist, some contemporary paraphrasing of the scripture quoted from Job 34 serves as good guidance:

Be intelligent and listen (v 16).

God is the One who brings about justice; and yet you condemn Him (v 17).

God condemns unfair rulers (v 18).

God created us all; He does not play favorites, whether rich or poor (v 19).

Even powerful rulers die in the darkness of night, when they least expect it, just like the rest of the world (v 20).

God effortlessly watches every step we take (v 21).

Not one evil person can hide (v 22).

God removes mighty leaders and puts others in their places without seeking advice (v 24).

These Biblical references and insights, as well as others presented hereafter, are offered to help create awareness of your life choices within the contemporary political setting. I don't mean the life designed and prescribed by this world, but the eternal one given to you by God.

Since the fall of man described in Genesis, human beings have continually chased riches, power, fame, and many other indulgences. Early humanity was generally driven by passions and had little or no interest in God. Their desires were byproducts of survival and self-gratification, which typically manifested as greed, lust, and violence–the hallmarks of primal instinct.

Be absolutely certain of this: sharing the same traits as our primitive ancestors is not a "good look" for anyone. At the end of our lives, who will God meet? Will He meet a champion of love or a self-serving cave dweller?

According to Hebrews 10:31 (NASB), *"It is a terrifying thing to fall into the hands of the living God."*

Based on that verse alone, I'm pretty sure the self-serving cave dweller might have a really bad first day in the afterlife.

As Americans, and as one nation under God, wouldn't it make sense to reclaim what God endowed us with? Should it be okay that Christian children aren't allowed to pray in our public schools while Muslim kids are able to worship freely? Where is the inclusion Democrats encourage? Does it not apply to Christians and conservative thinkers?

If there was a real spirit of inclusion and community, all opinions would matter. No one would be judged or alienated for wanting to keep what they earn, choose to eat, or that they drive a car that runs on gas.

In 1962, the U.S. Supreme court banned school-sponsored prayer in public schools, saying that it violated the First Amendment. Because of this, our school children are now denied the tradition of prayer. It is a terrible shame to watch the new political agenda take hold of every aspect of our lives. Sadly, in most places today, believers and conservatives are marginalized and treated as idiots.

Other than God's inevitable disappointment with mankind, it's difficult to forecast the long-term social results of this new brand of inclusive thinking. While inclusion itself is a generally positive concept, the forced inclusion of alternative culture is a dangerous experiment. This is what modern Democrats are doing without any apparent concern for where it will eventually lead us.

Together with the news media, film makers, and television studios, the Democrats are creating an illusion of diverse mainstream life. Even though this carefully crafted fantasy has no roots in reality, most people accept it as an accurate depiction of modern life. Consider the current mix of movies, television shows, news programs, and even the accompanying advertisements. They all follow the same formula for propagating the illusion of diversity and inclusion.

It appears as if everything we see on a daily basis defies the actual demographics. In fact, if a visitor from another planet were to prepare a report about Earth, it might submit that most people are gay or have gay friends and neighbors.

Regrettably, the extraterrestrial observer would not be alone in the misconception. People of all ages, races, and religions have submitted to the illusion without ever looking to the statistics and demanding balance.

According to The Williams Report,[5] the LGBT population is represented in the range of four-and-a-half percent of our population, while GLAAD (an American non-governmental media monitoring organization founded in 1985 by LGBT people in the media) recently reported that over ten percent of scripted characters on prime-time television were LGBTQ.[6] Obviously, this is a gratuitous misrepresentation of reality, and it's only going to expand.

Here's another important question. There are millions of evangelical Christians in the United States. Why aren't these Christians represented by a proportionate number of characters on television and in the movies? This misrepresentation should be embarrassing to those being depicted at exaggerated levels and insulting to those watching. If neither feels either, then perhaps they don't understand the underlying agenda.

Actors are being exploited for their sexual preferences, ethnicity, and/or religion, while the audience is being exposed to political programming. This is about control and not the purported social justice narrative. The Democratic Party and its media counterparts employ these tactics to systematically desensitize the masses. As this is accomplished, the support base will grow until most people are either indifferent or too ashamed to stand up for Christian values. Once this happens, the Party will have unprecedented power, which could conceivably last indefinitely.

Part of the strategy is to brand everything as a social disparity where all are shamed into thinking that the conservative response is inappropriate and insensitive. While the long-term results are still uncertain, social programming is already making its initial impact on future generations.

Radically, adolescents exposed to this new culture have a corrupted sense of sexual development. Naturally, kids on the threshold of sexual maturity are riddled with questions. Since the new social programming begins to reach children as toddlers, kids develop an awareness of alternative lifestyle options. In these formative years, they are exposed to television shows and movies that feature same-sex couples, transgender characters, and other LGBTQ protagonists. These shows are considered age-appropriate and seem harmless to most parents who casually submit their kids to this brainwashing.

As a child enters puberty, it is possible for him or her to believe they have a certain sexual orientation based on a primal hormonal experience. If conditioned to recognize alternative versions of sexual preference as socially acceptable, the adolescent is predisposed to confirm a chance experience as absolute orientation. From there, it's simply a matter of parental, peer, and societal affirmation.

Similarly, if a five-year-old boy puts on his mom's heels or six-year-old girl plays with dad's tie, tomorrow's parents may automatically assume transsexuality and encourage progression. Commonly, in its most simple form, the boy in heels just wants to be taller, and the girl is simply playing dress-up.

While it can be possible that the boy might be exhibiting homosexual tendencies, that's not the point. The point is that it is not for society, or even the boy himself, to decide. It is not a choice at all; sexual preference is an organic inclination which one finds extremely difficult to resist.

Believing in God means that each distinct sexual orientation has its own set of moral and physical boundaries. Fundamentally, alternative orientations require abstinence, while heterosexuality requires fortitude. Regardless of orientation, humans fail constantly, but the modern Democratic Party is actively encouraging failure by commoditizing sexual preferences.

The liberal mainstream has a game plan for our children and grandchildren. They are programming future generations to celebrate each other's defiance of God. Morals are optional. If it feels good, do whatever you want. The masses are being fooled by lies disguised as sensitivity. A rising star in the Democratic Party is Alexandria Ocasio-Cortez. At the Mexican border she claimed to see children in cages and drinking from toilets. She, of course, blamed President Trump. She labeled these detention centers as concentration camps.

Pastor Spargimino wrote recently (January 2020) in the *Prophetic Observer*, "This darling of the socialists said nothing about how America's border crisis is profiting a huge international criminal operation exploiting children while benefiting Mexican drug cartels, smugglers, and human traffickers who are reaping a fortune selling countless women and children into the sex slavery world."[7]

The bottom line is that Satan knows he will destroy our nation if he destroys the family.

The nuclear family, consisting of a father, mother, and children, is being undermined by the liberal mainstream. Leftist lawmakers are not interested in Biblical truths about family and fashion legislation around lies. Bob Glaze, in an October 2018 article featured in *Prophetic Observer* states, "The greatest place to incubate untruths is politics."

Truth leads to freedom, but lies lead to bondage. Regrettably, lies often seem like freedom, and this type of false freedom is better defined as rebellion. Why are so many people living in open rebellion? Christ says in Matthew 24:37-39 that end times would be "just like the days of Noah." People would rather chase pleasure by following Satan than live free and serve God.

If we review Genesis concerning the conditions of humanity during Noah's times, we see the following:

Man continued to reject God's instructions and became even more corrupt. God said (Genesis 6:5), *"The Lord saw the wickedness of man was great in the earth, and every intent of the thoughts of his heart was on evil continually."* There was no shame, no looking to God, only evil 24/7. The people ruined themselves and did not care.

Violence followed lawlessness. Jewish writers believed this violence developed because of too much ease, too much free time. The old saying, "An idle mind is the devil's workshop," seems appropriate for this time.

Jesus says in the 24th chapter of Matthew that in the last days people will be eating, drinking, and getting married, simply living life with no regard for God.

There are many similarities between Noah's day and our present day. For instance:

Corruption. Congress's care of Social Security is a joke. The US deficit is expected to reach $375 billion in 2025, which is clearly a violation of public trust. In Noah's day *"Every desire of man's heart was on evil"* (Proverbs 29:2).

Murder. Slaughter of babies through abortion. Is there anything more evil than taking a human life?

Noah's world was corrupt, with men and women seeking pleasure seeking at every turn. Today is worse. Our focus is on money, drugs, sex, and so on. Life is all about pleasure with little or no thought of the Lord.

CHAPTER SEVEN

UNDERSTANDING THE SIGNS OF THE TIMES

J esus said, "When it is evening, you say, '*It will be* fair weather, for the sky is red.' And in the morning, '*There will be* a storm today, for the sky is red and threatening.' Do you know how to discern the appearance of the sky, but cannot *discern* the signs of the times?" (Matthew 16:2-3)

We are witnesses to evil in action. Protest groups hiding behind names such as "Women's March" are mostly funded by globalist George Soros. He is funding riots, marches, and more to promote "an open society," a society that promotes population control, global governance, and reallocation of money from our middle class to the poor. Soros is also busy in Europe and the Middle East.

The Bible tells us, *"This know also, that in the last days perilous times shall come"* (2 Timothy 3:1 KJV).

The stage is being set for a one-world government. The Bible compares the nations and peoples of the earth to a restless sea (Daniel 7:2, Revelation 13:1). People like Mr. Soros are playing into the hands of Satan, whose evil goal is to enslave humanity. A clearer picture of what is to come is stated in Proverbs 29:16 NKJ: *"When the wicked are multiplied, transgressions increase."* In other words, the more sinners the more sin!

Who is Mr. Soros? What kind of person supports positions that are radical to the Christian mindset? He is one of the world's leading philanthropists. He has given $32 billion to fund "Open-society foundations" and founded the Central European University for the study of social sciences. He is passionate in what he believes. He has supported people across the globe irrespective of race or creed. His goal is to help those who have been overlooked or shunned by the mainstream. This includes drug users, sex workers, and others across the globe.

His reason for such help comes from his own experience. Born in Hungary, Soros lived through the Nazi occupation of 1944-1945, which resulted in the murder of 500,000 Jews. After the war, he worked in London as a part-time night club waiter to support his studies at the London School of Economics. He emigrated to the United States in 1956 and made his fortune here.

His open-society thinking was derived from his studies under Karl Poppers, who argued "no philosophy or ideology is the final arbiter of truth, and that societies can only flourish when they allow for democratic governance, freedom of expression, and respect for individual rights."

I believe Mr. Soros means well. Had he believed the "final arbiter of truth is God, and not a society for Democratic governance," it would make perfect sense: Truth belongs to the Builder of the world and the Creator of man, not some democratic group of people who have no clue about Christ or what He did to get mankind back.

In ancient days, people on earth made choices according to their senses. People were addicts of their senses, much like today. I once read that there is no other area of desire – outside of breathing and living – as powerful and intoxicating as sex. In the pre-flood world, sex was a narcotic, a natural function ordained by God for procreation but turned into an evil addiction. It's easy to envision a world filled with sinful cravings. In

44

the days of Noah, mankind thought and acted on these cravings 24 hours a day, 7 days a week

Engaging in sexual promiscuity, rape, pedophilia, and much more, people in Noah's day acted out every evil the Bible warns against. Consider God's reaction to open sexual sin found in Genesis 18. God literally destroyed Sodom and Gomorrah for their misdeeds.

Today we have the word *transgendered*. Walt Heyer is a psychiatrist and college professor who underwent gender surgery from male to female at age forty-two. He lived as "Laura Jensen" for eight years. At that point, he realized his unresolved childhood trauma was behind the desire to escape into another gender.

After many hours of psychological counseling, Heyer's desire to be a woman dissipated. He built his life anew and has married a biological woman. He has now been married for twenty-two years and is very happy. Because of the changes that have taken place in our society over the past few years, he wants to share his story with others, so they don't make the same mistake he did. He says, "I feel compelled to share this hope with others by speaking out against the lie that regret is rare and to expose the lies of the sex-change movement from an insider's perspective."

What changed for Heyer was the explosion in the number of children and adolescents diagnosed with "gender dysphoria" and the stranglehold excluding other treatment options. He has advised parents to work with professional counseling to identify the cause of the stress and cautioned these parents to avoid those who encourage gender change. He says parents are in the best position to identify the root cause of their children's' stress and urges them to avoid "gender clinics" at all costs.

Most individuals believe God is love and that He is merciful. But God is also just. The misconception of many is that God thinks the way we think. This is entirely incorrect. God is holy, and this holiness dictates His every action. His holiness is who He is, His character. He is completely different from us. And He will not tolerate it if we thumb our noses at Him and say, "I don't like the way You made me. I don't want to be a man (or woman). I want to be the other gender instead."

We are not gods and we cannot remake the world into our own image. God has put boundaries in place that we are not to cross. Our sexual identity is one of these.

In his 2019 speech to the 74th Session of the United Nations General Assembly, President Trump stated, "The essential divide that runs all around the world and throughout history is once again thrown into stark relief. It is the divide between those whose thirst for control deludes them into thinking they are destined to rule over others and those people and nations who want only to rule themselves."

As the President says, controlling others against their will is incompatible with God's desire for mankind. This flies in the face of the expectations and desires of globalists who believe they are destined to rule the world.

President Trump went on to remind us that 100 million people have been killed by socialism and communism and that these regimes today have an added and more powerful dimension called modern technology.

The number of nations who hate the United States is growing.

Imagine what would happen if an enemy detonated a nuclear device over the United States. Within a year, over ninety percent of Americans would perish. Supermarkets would have no food to sell. Trucks and cars would have no fuel. Our defense system would be rendered useless. We must vote to keep America strong so that this tragic scenario never takes place.

Remember, you are responsible for protecting this nation, including your children and grandchildren. You have a weapon (your vote), but you have no weapon against hunger or thirst. Men and women died in previous wars for us to have freedom, food, water, and a good life.

When was the last time you thanked God that you were born in this country? We have been blessed beyond our understanding.

CHAPTER EIGHT

WAKE UP!

Who are you listening to? What is God saying to you?

If you are standing on the platform of the Democratic Party, I sincerely believe that you are supporting issues God calls sin. Consider abortion. How can one claim to be a proponent of Christianity while supporting the killing of innocent unborn children. Obviously, there are an overwhelming number of political positions that conflict with a basic belief in God. Most reside in the Democratic Party.

President Kennedy's party platform is not the same as that of former President Obama. I am not saying everyone needs to be a Republican. I am saying that, while all people are flawed, it is critical to align oneself with those who have a sense of morality.

The 1956 Democratic platform called for voting rights, desegregation of public schools and equal employment opportunities – but not for same-sex marriage, abortion, and equal rights for homosexuals.

The Republican Party has not changed much through recent years. The GOP favors conservatism, a strong national defense, lower taxes, and less federal intervention in our free-market economy.

As a conservative and a proponent of a strong military, I believe we stand to lose our way of life if we do not continue to strengthen our military.

Most Americans think we are the most powerful nation on the planet. At one time they would have been correct. However, while currently stronger under President Trump, we are not where we need to be for a safe future.

Because I believe everything the Bible says, I also believe that we must align ourselves militarily with Israel. To go against Israel is to go against God.

In Genesis 12:3, God says of Israel, *"And I will bless those who bless you, And the one who curses you I will curse. And in you all the families of the earth will be blessed."*

Notice how many times God says "I will." This chapter explains how God promised Abraham a land, a nation, and a blessing. Consider what happened to the nations who chose to ignore this scripture. Time and time again, the nations that surround Israel have chosen to attack her. They have had more soldiers, more weapons, and more power. But Israel has always prevailed and always will. This happened throughout history.

Soon after the Greeks desecrated the altar in the Temple at Jerusalem, they were conquered by Rome. Subsequently, the Roman army under Titus destroyed the Temple in 70 A.D., and they thereafter fell to multiple German tribes. Spain also fell after the Inquisition against the Jews. Poland fell after the "Pogroms" (the word *pogroms* is from a Russian word meaning to destroy). In modern days, Adolf Hitler decided to exterminate the Jews. He also said his Third Reich would last for 1,000 years. Nazi Germany was long ago swept away, but Israel and the Jewish people are thriving.

The British Empire lost its power after turning its back on its promise to the Jews.

Numbers 24:9 also states, *"The nation is like a mighty lion; when it is sleeping, no one dares wake it. Whoever blesses Israel will be blessed, and whoever curses Israel will be cursed."*

In Psalm 122, we read: *"Pray for the peace of Jerusalem: they that love thee shall prosper."*

We cannot be led astray by politicians who want to cut support for Israel, or who call for an economic boycott because of Israel's supposed mistreatment of the Palestinian people.

Several years ago, a man named Bill Koenig wrote a book, Eye to Eye,[8] in which he shows how the fortunes of the United States are dependent on our treatment of Israel. When we bless Israel, we are blessed. When we move against Israel, our blessings are taken away. After reading Koenig's book, you will see that one of the worst things the United States can do is pressure Israel to give up some of the land that God gave them nearly 4,000 years ago.

Here are just some of the occurrences Koenig records:

August 20, 1991: As President George Bush opens the Madrid Conference, which will ask Israel to give up land in return for peace in the Middle East, a huge storm develops in the North Atlantic Ocean. The storm travels 1,000 miles from east to west – the opposite of the path storms in this region usually follow – and sends 35-foot-tall waves crashing onto the coast of New England, including the President's home at Kennebunkport, Maine.

January 16, 1994: President Bill Clinton travels to Geneva to meet with Syria's President Hafez el-Assad. The two men are scheduled to talk about a peace treaty that is built around the nation of Israel giving the Golan Heights back to the Palestinians. The next day, the Northridge Earthquake hits Southern

California, killing 72 people, leaving an estimated 9,000 injured and causing $25 billion worth of property damage.

September 28, 1998: As Secretary of State Madeline Albright puts the finishing touches on a peace agreement that will ask Israel to give up 13 percent of Judea and Samaria, Hurricane George charges into the Gulf Coast, causing $1 billion worth of damage.

May 3, 1999: On the day Yasser Arafat is scheduled to declare a Palestinian state with Jerusalem as its capital, with the blessing of the United States government, the most powerful tornadoes on record wreak havoc in Oklahoma and Kansas. Winds of more than 300 miles per hour are recorded. Forty deaths are recorded in Oklahoma, with at least five more fatalities in Wichita, Kansas, and hundreds of houses are damaged or destroyed.

August 2005: During this month, many Jewish families were evicted from their homes in the Gaza Strip as part of the Israeli government's Disengagement Plan for the region. The plan was developed for the most part, by the Administration of George W. Bush, and our government applied pressure on the Israelis to accept it. American television networks interrupted their coverage of what was happening in Israel for a special news bulletin: a hurricane – named Katrina – was forming in the Atlantic Ocean.

These are just a few of the powerful examples you can find in Koenig's book. I think it's clear that we must vote for men and women who love Israel, as Donald Trump clearly does. Remember that he moved the American embassy to Jerusalem after years of delay on the part of other presidents because they feared that the move would make enemies for us in the Arab world. But why would we turn our backs on our friends to appease people who already hate us?

And, by the way, the truth is that Israelis and Palestinians are half brothers.

Let me briefly explain. The Bible tells us that Esau and Jacob were twin brothers born to Rebekah and Isaac. In Genesis 25 we read that Rebekah asked God why there was such turmoil in her stomach. The Lord answered saying that "two nations are in your womb, and two peoples from within you will be separated; one people will be stronger than the other, and the older will serve the younger."

Esau was the first to be born. Then Jacob emerged grasping Esau's heel. (Jacob means "supplanter.") As first-born Esau received the birthright, the blessing passed on from Abraham through Isaac. (The entire blessing can be read in Genesis 17:5-8.)

In Genesis 25:29-34, we read that Esau traded his birthright to Jacob for a bowl of lentil soup. Esau was hungry and said, "I am about to die, what good is the birthright to me?" This event led to a great deal of strife between the two men. It seems that they never got along and neither have their descendants.

Eventually, Esau married an Ishmaelite and moved to Seir, the rugged, mountain country of the Edomites. After a few years, the Edomites became a large and powerful tribe. Esau lived out his life in an area of red-walled canyons. According to one school of thought, today's Arab peoples are the descendants of the Edomite. My own study of the subject has convinced me this is true – although others believe that Isaac's half-brother Ishmael is the ancestor of today's Arabs.

What does this ancient history have to do with us in 2020? Plenty.

The far-reaching consequences of Esau's desire to seek his own way resulted in rejecting God's wisdom and choosing a self-centered approach to living. Esau hardened his heart against a godly lifestyle. Hebrews 12:16 says of him, "see that no one is sexually immoral, or is godless like Esau."

Like many today, Esau was not a bad person. He was not a thief. He was not perverted, but he was basically godless. There's no record of Esau blaspheming or talking evil about God; he never considered God at all.

When you are standing in line at the polls, please consider asking God how you should vote. None of us should think we have all the answers in ourselves. We don't. Don't sell your birthright by ignoring the scriptures. Don't follow Esau's ways by turning your back on God. God will punish sin. There is no statute of limitations on sin. God loves you and wants the best for you, so choose life and not death.

CHAPTER NINE

VOTE TO PROTECT AMERICA

Donald Trump and the Republicans want to build a wall along the Mexican border, to protect our country from the flood of illegal aliens that desire to come into this country.

Joe Biden and the Democrats plan to stop work on the wall, and thereby make it easier for illegals to gain entry into the United States.

How you vote depends on what will happen to the wall – and therefore to the United States as a whole. I believe, for several reasons, that we must vote to build the wall.

Why? Am I prejudiced against Mexicans?

Not at all.

But just look what the drug cartels have done in that country. Hundreds of thousands of innocent civilians have been killed in drug wars between various cartels. Headless corpses have been hung from railroad bridges in many communities as a warning to any who would defy the cartels.

Thousands of bodies have been found in mass graves. People have been burned alive, skinned, and killed in other gruesome ways. According to some reports, 80 percent of Mexico is controlled by the cartels rather than the government.

We cannot allow these criminals to get a foothold in the United States, or similar atrocities and bloodletting will soon be happening here.

Remember, it is not just ordinary people in search of a better life who will come through our open borders. Without a wall, more deadly drugs, including heroin and fentanyl will poor into this country. So will thousands of young girls who are being trafficked by sexual predators. And, of course, we will be opening ourselves up to terrorists associated with Islamic State, Al Qaeda and other organizations.

In his book, *Defend the Border and Save Lives*, Tom Homan, Former Director of ICE, writes about the importance of a wall along our Southern border:[9] "Without a wall, our border is a revolving door for bad guys. Gang members and those with criminal records don't usually drive through legal ports of entry, because they know our database continues to improve. One particular arrest from my career comes to mind. The man was missing several fingers on his right hand. He told me he'd lost them in a farming accident. I arrested him around nine o'clock in the morning on the east side of the port of entry, processed him—an experienced agent could process an illegal alien in just twenty minutes—and drove him back to the border. A couple hours later, I arrested him coming over the west side of the port of entry. We processed him again. We sent him back. That afternoon, a sensor went off in an area outside my patrol, but the other agent was busy. As I drove up to the man, he turned to me and started laughing. By now, we had a pretty good routine, and I processed him in record time.

"Later that afternoon, an agent walked into the office with an arrestee. "Did you just arrest him?" I asked. "Yeah, do you know this guy?" "You could say that. I arrested him three times today."

You see how easy it is for illegal aliens to gain access to the United States without a wall to stop them? Even when our government stops them and sends them back to Mexico, they just keep on coming back. We are almost defenseless against them.

Why don't Democrats favor a wall on our southern border? Apparently, they don't think it's critical to our safety. They are not concerned about an invasion, nor do they imagine one in the future. As far back as 3500 BCE, countries and cities have built walls to protect their people. China built the Great Wall, and the ancient Greeks built walls, towers, and gates.

What is God's thinking on building walls? God instructed Nehemiah to rebuild the wall around Jerusalem to protect its citizens from enemy attack. Nehemiah asked Artaxerxes if he could rebuild the wall in Jerusalem and his request was granted.

The Trump wall is not intended to keep all immigrants out, but to prohibit those who would do us harm from coming in. Both Old and New Testaments remind us of our responsibility to protect our own as well as strangers (immigrants). You see, we too were immigrants. The people who learn our language, pay their fair share of taxes, and abide by the laws of our land are more than welcome here.

More dangers facing America

We must clean up our cities.

Imagine you are sitting in the comfortable suburbs of America thinking this will not affect you. Your family is safe from the city filth. You would be 100 percent wrong. Filth and disease are followed by rats. The Hepatitis-E virus is now on the list of dangerous pathogens that may be transmitted from rats to humans. This virus is estimated to infect twenty million people worldwide, resulting in 3.3 million people showing symptoms each year.

According to the World Health Organization (WHO), rats caused 44,000 deaths in 2015, which accounted for 3.3 percent of all deaths from viral hepatitis.[10] These rodents breed year-round with females usually having five litters a year, which reach sexual maturity in five weeks. One pair of brown rats can produce as many as 2,000 rats in a year if left unchecked.

This issue will not go away on its own. New York had an interesting solution. Brooklyn introduced opossums in the city in 2007, but this created another epidemic. The opossums were released to kill rats, but the wild opossums destroyed gardens, threatened small dogs, and terrified the young and elderly. At the end of the day, the opossums created new problems without reducing the rodent population.

Rats may be winning in New York, but Chicago is a different story. The rat problem there is so bad Chicago has been named the Rat Capital of America. In 2000, coyotes were released to combat the rat infestation. Today, there are about 2,000 coyotes roaming the streets of Chicago.

Since the beginning of this research project there have not been any reports of bites to humans–until 2019. I say this to drive home the point that we are not helping the poor of our streets; we are creating a much larger problem which could lead to a resurgence of the bubonic plague. The "Black Death" that killed over fifty million people in the Middle Ages is still around today, and is rising swiftly.

Immigration is another great concern for Americans who care about our future. Democrats support an easier path to immigration. Obama's Dream Act, which opposes state laws targeting immigrants, ensures that young people who were born here can become citizens. Democrats are more sympathetic to sanctuary cities. They firmly believe immigration is not a problem but an aspect of American character and our shared history. Their mantra is "seek to embrace, not erase or attack immigrants."

As might be expected, the majority of immigrants vote for the Democratic Party. As of 2015 the USA has approximately forty-seven million immigrants, about fifteen percent of our population.[11] Most of these individuals live in one of the many sanctuary cities sprinkled throughout the USA. Basically, these cities limit their cooperation with the national government's effort to enforce immigration laws. They do this to protect low priority immigrants from deportation.

CHAPTER TEN

VOTE OUT OF YOUR COMFORT ZONE

Some people vote Democratic – or Republican – because that's what their parents did. Others think they are compelled to vote a certain way because of their race or religion. For example, they believe that all Catholics vote Democratic – or that all blacks vote Democratic. To those who believe such things, I have an important bit of advice:

Think for yourself and be willing to vote out of your comfort zone.

Times have changed and so have the parties.

For example, prior to the 1960s, the South was solidly Democratic. After all, the Republicans were the party of Abraham Lincoln, and Lincoln was the commander-in-chief of the Union Army during the Civil War. But times have changed, and millions throughout the south are now in agreement with the conservative views of the Republican Party on state's rights, taxes, the military and many other issues.

Now, let's consider some of these groups who have consistently voted for one party.

Consider the Jewish allegiance to the Democratic Party. Immigrating to America by the millions between 1880 and 1920 primarily to escape the anti-Semitism sweeping across

Europe, Jews found refuge in the five-points slums of New York on the Lower East Side. Life there was miserable. They worked for pennies and saw no way out.

In 1911 the Triangle Shirtwaist Factory in Greenwich Village employed mostly Italian and Jewish women. Doors were typically locked to keep workers from taking unauthorized breaks and to prevent theft. When a fire broke out on March 25, 146 men, women, and children perished from the fire itself, smoke inhalation, or from jumping or falling to their deaths. Forty-six of these were Jewish women.

Following the tragedy, the entire Jewish community erupted in anger and united to join the movement to unionize New York's garment industry. This move was strongly endorsed by the Democratic Party and, conversely, resisted by the Republican Party. This emotional stance became part of the Jewish psyche and, in my opinion, was the right thing to do at that time in history.

As stated elsewhere, the Democratic Party at that time was completely different from today's Party. Democrats of that era supported the "little guy." The Republican Party of that era was the "Rich Man's Party." Jews and Democrats were now joined at the hip. The Democratic Party was perceived as supporting justice for the oppressed. This perspective continues to this day.

But if you are Jewish, I urge you to remember that in today's world, the Republican Party is more likely to stand up for the nation of Israel. It was the Republicans, for the most part, who invited Benjamin Netanyahu to address the United States Congress in May of 2015. It is the Republicans who vote to continue and increase American support for Israel. And, as I mentioned previously, it was Donald Trump who moved the American embassy from Tel Aviv to Jerusalem, despite the objections of Muslims throughout the world.

And if you are Jewish, don't make the mistake of thinking the nation of Israel has nothing to do with you. It is a symbol to the world of the strength of the Jewish people. It is a reminder that they will never again be victimized by monstrous men like Adolf Hitler, and that they have friends and allies who will stand with them and support them.

The Catholic Context:

Do Catholics vote as directed by the Pope? David Carlin attempts to answer this question in his book, *Can a Catholic be a Democrat?*[12] In a section titled *How the Party I Loved Became the Enemy of My Religion,* he writes, "Both parties endorse policies or engage in activities that contradict some or many Catholic teachings about abortion, poverty, immigration, war and peace, or other issues of life and justice."

As I was born and raised Catholic, I'm able to share some thoughts regarding the Catholic perspective.

Back in the 1940s, if you were a good catholic you were a Democrat. As an American Catholic you were joined at the hip with Rome and the Pope. All this changed in the sixties. Italians were no longer just laborers, but were doctors, lawyers, judges educated in politics, God-fearing, church-going people.

During that time, a young, energetic Irish-Catholic Senator named John F. Kennedy came into the political arena. He came from a wealthy family headed by Joseph P. Kennedy, former British Ambassador and successful businessman. Senator Kennedy, a Democrat, was elected President of the United States in 1960. His policies were more Republican then President Reagan's. After Kennedy's assassination, the Party became more secular. It became acceptable to kill unborn babies as well as flaunt one's sexuality.

This transformation caused the breaking of the alliance between Catholics and the Democratic Party. How will the Catholic block cast their vote, considering that Catholics now comprise 27 percent of the national vote? When it comes to same-sex marriage and abortion, the Catholics are in alignment with Protestant Evangelicals. If you are Catholic, you need to understand that you are not called to select the party with the most positive positions. Rather, you are choosing between life and death.

Since God has not changed His mind on abortion or homosexuality, your decision, as a Catholic, must be in line with God's moral code. This choice is not about party affiliation. If you want to vote for policies that are consistent with God's thinking, you cannot pull the Democratic lever.

Carlin states that the "modern, secularist Democratic Party has become the enemy of Catholicism." He shatters the excuses Catholic Democratic politicians employ in a vain attempt to reconcile their faith and their votes. With what Carlin calls the "political equivalent of a broken heart," he examines his own political conscience. Carlin's arguments challenge all religious voters to ask themselves the same questions.

The Muslim Context:

The 2000 Presidential election saw George W. Bush delivering a socially conservative message to the Muslim community. It was later determined that he received 42 percent of their vote, versus 31 percent that went to Mr. Gore.

American Muslims are gaining traction. In spite of President Trump's tweets and rhetoric against the Muslim community, two Muslim women (Rashida Tlaib and Ilhan Omar) were elected to the House of Representatives. Approximately 65 percent of Muslims are expected to vote for the Democratic nominee.

This past year's congressional elections saw an increase in the number of votes cast. Pew reports about 3.5 million Muslims now live in America. This picture is expected to change quickly with the Muslim share doubling by the middle of the century.

Younger Muslims have been Americanized. They are much more liberal about cultural questions like abortion and gay rights, thus they shun Republican "family values." African-American Muslims are predicted to be far left with regard to their voting choices.

The African American Context:

Just as the American South was once solidly in the Democratic Camp, African-Americans were solidly Republican. That changed in the 1930s when Franklin D. Roosevelt was elected, and black allegiance to the Democratic Party has grown stronger ever since. In recent years, blacks have overwhelmingly voted for Bill Clinton, Al Gore, John Kerry, Barack Obama and Hillary Clinton. Joe Biden will undoubtedly get the majority of the black vote in 2020.

Since 1992, no candidate has won the Democratic nomination for president without winning a majority of the black vote. Black voters accounted for approximately one of every four primary ballots cast in 2020.

Walter Williams, an economist, commentator, syndicated columnist, and professor at George Mason University wrote in a recent article,[13] "While it may not be popular to say in the wake of the recent social disorder, the true plight of black people has little or nothing to do with the police or what has been called 'systemic racism.' Instead, we need to look at the responsibilities of those running our big cities."

Mr. Williams, an African-American himself, goes on to explain that in many of the cities (St. Louis, Baltimore, Oakland,

Chicago, Memphis, Atlanta, Newark, Buffalo, and Philadelphia) blacks are mayors, police chiefs, school superintendents, and largely comprise city councils. The common denominator for these cities is that they have been run by liberal Democrats for decades.

Today, fifty-two House members are African-American, nine have served in the Senate, and three are governors. Mr. Williams makes the following point, "Today's black America has significant political power at all levels of government. Yet what has that meant for a large segment of the black population?"

He goes on to mention that Democrat-controlled cities have the poorest public education despite their enormous school budgets. He goes on to detail the academic disasters in Baltimore and other Democrat-run cities. Violent crime develops, causing many of the good, hard-working, productive people to leave, which results in cities losing their economic base. Baltimore's population in 1950 was nearly one million people. Today it's 590,000. St. Louis declined from 856,000 (1950) to less than 294,000.

Mr. Williams further states, "Academic Liberals, civil rights advocates and others blamed the exodus on racism 'White Flight' to the suburbs to avoid blacks." He goes on to say blacks have been fleeing at higher rates than whites. Based on this, one could easily surmise that these cities are not offering safety, security, opportunity, or better standards of living for African-Americans.

If you are black, I urge you to carefully consider all this before you pull the lever in your voting booth. It is okay for you to break with tradition. We are all Americans and we need to stand together for the good of our country. Ask yourself which party has a better plan for cleaning up our cities, for fighting crime, for fighting poverty by providing good jobs, for promoting family values? All of these things must be vitally important to you as a black American, and should be reason enough to take a closer look at the Republican Party.

All of the Above as Americans:

There are obviously many races and ethnic groups on this planet, and all are divided by distinct genetic origins. While some races distinguish themselves further through sharing a common religious belief, this is not always true. Race is purely genetic.

Since the beginning of time, slight variations within the human genome have prompted competition. In fact, anyone with a sense of human history should agree that racial groups continually vie for dominance.

Within this context, it is reasonable to suggest that each race tends to promote its own kind while being inherently critical of others. Regrettably, this was not God's intention. It was man's own folly that caused the subtle branching and resulting lack of harmony. He only made one race: the human race.

America, in many ways, was the first place to lay the foundation for harmonious existence. It wasn't perfect and there were many sad casualties, but the concept was there. This country was intended to be a place where all people could come and live freely. It was envisioned as a melting pot where races, ethnicities, and beliefs would meld into a singular American culture. Essentially, the creation of an "American" race would flower into a successful union of free people.

Somewhere along the way, this concept was lost. The melting pot became more like a salad bowl. We will never have true harmony if we remain a salad. In this flavor arena, tomatoes will always compete with the carrots, while the onions will overpower everything if not balanced with cucumber. Cover it all with dressing to make everything works together, and voila! –it's delicious. Still, just below the coating of creamy ranch, there's conflict.

The same applies in today's culture. We may think covering everyone with Americana dressing equates to a highly functioning society, but it doesn't. By now, almost 245 years after July 4, 1776, Americans should have more in common with each other. We should be sharing a more uniform sense of style, speech, and behavior. On a daily basis, one should expect an overtly American response from anyone they encounter. This reaction to each other should be rooted in a common respect for the pursuit of happiness. Above all, Americans should have developed a sense of team.

Unfortunately, we're just not there. Even more regrettable, the Democrats are actually against this vision of unity.

CHAPTER ELEVEN

VOTING AND THE ETERNAL SOUL

I magine a bird gathering sand from the beaches up and down the east coast. He picks up one grain, once a year, and flies to the west coast where he drops it on a Pacific beach. By the time every grain is moved, Eternity will have only begun.

Many millennials will laugh at the above illustration. According to the Pew Research Center, four out of ten millennials claim to be religiously unaffiliated. There is mounting evidence that the younger generation is leaving religion for good. The political ramifications of this are great, according to Daniel Cox, co-author of *Millennials Are Leaving Religion and Not Coming Back.*[14]

"For one thing, religious involvement is associated with a wide variety of positive social outcomes like increased interpersonal trust and civic engagement that are hard to reproduce in other ways. And this trend has obvious political implications. Whether people are religious is increasingly tied to—and even driven by—their political identities... And as even more Democrats lose their faith, that will only exacerbate the acrimonious rift between secular liberals and religious conservatives."

I am reminded of (Galatians 6:7), which says, *"Do not be deceived: God is not to be mocked. Whatever a man sows, he will reap in return."*

Mocked means to disrespect God. Psalm 74:22 tells us that mocking is the attitude of a foolish man. Proverbs 1:22 and 13:1 add that fools hate knowledge and are without a spirit of obedience, without wisdom, and without faith.

Those who mock God will also mock God's people. Mockery of God's prophets was commonplace (2 Chronicles 36:16).

Charles G. Finney wrote about the effects of mocking God.[15] "To mock God is to pretend to love and serve Him, when we do not; to act in a false manner, to be insincere and hypocritical in our professions, pretending to obey Him, love, serve, and worship Him, when we do not. Mocking God grieves the Holy Spirit, and sears the conscience; and the bands of sin become stronger and stronger. The heart becomes gradually hardened by such a process."

The Bible tells us in 2 Timothy 4:3 that a time is coming when people will not tolerate sound doctrine, but with itching ears they will accumulate for themselves teachers that suit their own passions.

Please recall what I said concerning eternity and your decisions being for life or death. Bear one important thought in mind: God loves you, and that is unchanging. His love was demonstrated at the cross. Jesus is so far above us. He is the Creator of everything we see. In comparison, we are little more than dogs, and yet He voluntarily shed His majesty to put on our humanity and died a miserable death so we could live and have eternal life. Paul says God did this for us, "so that your faith might not rest on human wisdom, but on God's power." (1 Corinthians 2:5)

This short book is not meant to be hurtful; it's meant to be truthful. My heart breaks for my family of mankind. We were not given life in order to squander it on carnal pleasures, but so we can love, honor, and obey our Creator in all things.

CHAPTER TWELVE

WHICH WAY WILL YOU GO?

Whether you like him or not, President Trump has America's best interests in mind. Yes, his tweets are annoying. Yes, his former womanizing days weren't what we consider presidential. Yes, he sometimes come across like a bull in a china shop. Yes, his mockery of someone's height or teeth is inappropriate. Yes, he is sensitive to criticism. And, yes, the rotation of personnel in his administration borders on ridiculous as does his rejection of the advice given to him by his handpicked team. He is flawed for sure, but so was King David, and so are we all.

However, the answers to the questions below are more important than all of the above.

Has President Trump delivered on his campaign promises?

Has Trump made America a safer place for our families?

Did he deliver on his promise to create more jobs?

Has America gained more respect in the world?

Will he continue to keep our safety foremost?

Did God tell David to attack Goliath?

How does this last question make sense even remotely in the context of this book?

Difficult trials reveal the true priorities of our faith.

God placed stories in the Bible so we can interpret what He wants us to learn. This narrative is all about trust. If nothing happens in this universe without God's consent, then Mr. Trump was not an accident. Like David, who was at times unfaithful and manipulative, President Trump has flaws. Yet God forgives. Every president we have had, whether good or bad, was God's choice for this nation at a certain time. I believe that Donald Trump is the man of the hour for America today.

In the book of Esther, we find the story of a young queen who was chosen to save the Jewish people from a murderous man named Haman. In order to rescue the Jews, Esther had to put her own life at risk. She was encouraged to be brave by her uncle, Mordecai, who told her, *"And who knows but that you have come to your royal position for such a time as this?"* (Esther 4:14) She acted as her uncle urged her to do and saved her fellow Jews from Haman's plot.

Similarly, I believe that Donald Trump has been called to lead America forward in our hour of trouble.

Can anyone relate to David's mistakes? As a young shepherd, David killed lions and bears, preparing him to meet the challenge of Goliath. Because of his faith in God, David was able to slay the giant. And just as David had defended his sheep against the marauders, he declared that he would not stand by and watch as the God of Israel was taunted and cursed by the heathen Goliath. God didn't need to tell David to kill Goliath. David knew it was the right thing to do. It's the same for President Trump. He sees the enemies (both internal and external) trying to kill the people that belong to God. And he's determined to do what is right.

Remember, God is still on the throne and still in control. He is allowing the pandemic, Locusts, abnormal weather patterns across the globe, etc, all to get us to focus on Him. Not ourselves, and our pleasures.

The Globalists see an opening and want to take America down. If that happens, the world economy will implode. Satan would love nothing more than to see this happen. He hates Americans because he knows that God loves us – because we have always stood with Israel.

Listen very carefully. Whether you like or hate Mr. Trump, know this for sure – God placed him in office to do His holy will. Satan knows prophecy and he knows the rapture is near, so keep your eyes on Christ and not on the chaos that surrounds you. Stay alert and concentrate on who will best protect your children, and grandchildren. Trump dislikes the globalists and will stop them every chance he can.

Trust me, their goal is more and more chaos. Look for more and more heartaches. Make no mistake, the globalists see an opportunity to get one of their own into the White House and they will pull out all the stops. Look for increased hatred throughout the world, especially against Jews and Christians. Look for larger riots and fewer and fewer people going to church.

This book was written with the love Christ demonstrated on the cross. It is written for those who want to have a relationship with the Lord. It is not a chastisement of your political affiliation; it is simply a call for you to consider your party and its platform and how it lines up with what God requires of man.

Keep one very important issue in mind: **Your citizenship is in heaven.** Philippians 3:20 says, *"For our citizenship is in heaven, from which also we eagerly await for our Savior, the Lord Jesus Christ."*

In other words, you are not going *to be*, you already *are* a citizen of heaven. As a citizen, you are automatically part of the Lord's priesthood. In ancient Israel priests were the privileged servants of God.

Before pulling the lever in your voting booth, please consider what I am trying to convey: Life is short; eternity is forever.

Second, remember you are not voting for a specific person; you are voting for the entire platform on which your candidate stands.

Third, voting is a right bestowed on you by the blood of many men and women who gave their lives for the privilege and freedom to vote.

Fourth, you cannot choose by saying you are in agreement with all the issues but one (abortion, for instance). Pulling the lever states to the world you are in favor of everything this political platform supports. Finally, and most important, before you leave your house or apartment to vote, pray to the Holy Spirit to give you guidance in your choices.

Therefore, choose wisely, it is your life-or-death decision for eternity.

END NOTES

1   Freitas, Donna, "The Happiness Effect," London: Oxford University Press, 2017, Pages XVI-XVII

2   Titus Flavius Josephus as quoted in Christian Forums.com on December 15, 2014, accessed on August 6, 2020

3   Stanley Kurtz, "Radical-in-Chief: Barack Obama and the Untold Story of American Socialism," New York: Simon & Schuster, 2010

4   Spargimino, Dr. Larry, The Prophetic Observer, published by the Southwest Radio Bible Church, January 2020

5   "Adult LGBT Population in the United States," williams institute.law.ucla.edu/publications, July 2020, accessed on August 7, 2020

6   "Study finds LGBTQ characters hit record high on network TV," ap.news.com, November 7, 2019, accessed on August 7, 2020

7   Spargimino, Dr. Larry, The Prophetic Observer, January 2020

8   Koenig, Bill, "Eye to Eye – Facing the Consequences of Dividing Israel," Springfield, MO, 21st Century Press, 2004

9   Homan, Tom, "Defend the Border and Save Lives," New York City: Center Street, 2020

10 www.who.intl/health info/mortalilty data/2016 accessed August 7, 2020

11 Wikipedia.com, "Immmigration to the United States," accessed August 7, 2020

12 Carlin, David, *Can a Catholic be a Democrat?* Sophia Institute Press, Manchester, N.H., 2006

13 Walter W. Williams, "The True Plight of Black Americans is not "systemic Racism," Capitolism Magazine, June 9, 2020

14 "Millennials are Leaving Religion and Not Coming Back," by Daniel Cox and Amelia Thomson-DeVeaux, fivethirtyeight. com/features, accessed August 8, 2020

15 gospeltruth.net, "Mocking God: A sermon delivered on Friday Evening, May 31, 1850 by Charlies G. Finney," accessed August 8, 2020

CPSIA information can be obtained
at www.ICGtesting.com
Printed in the USA
LVHW081121141020
668786LV00016B/1039